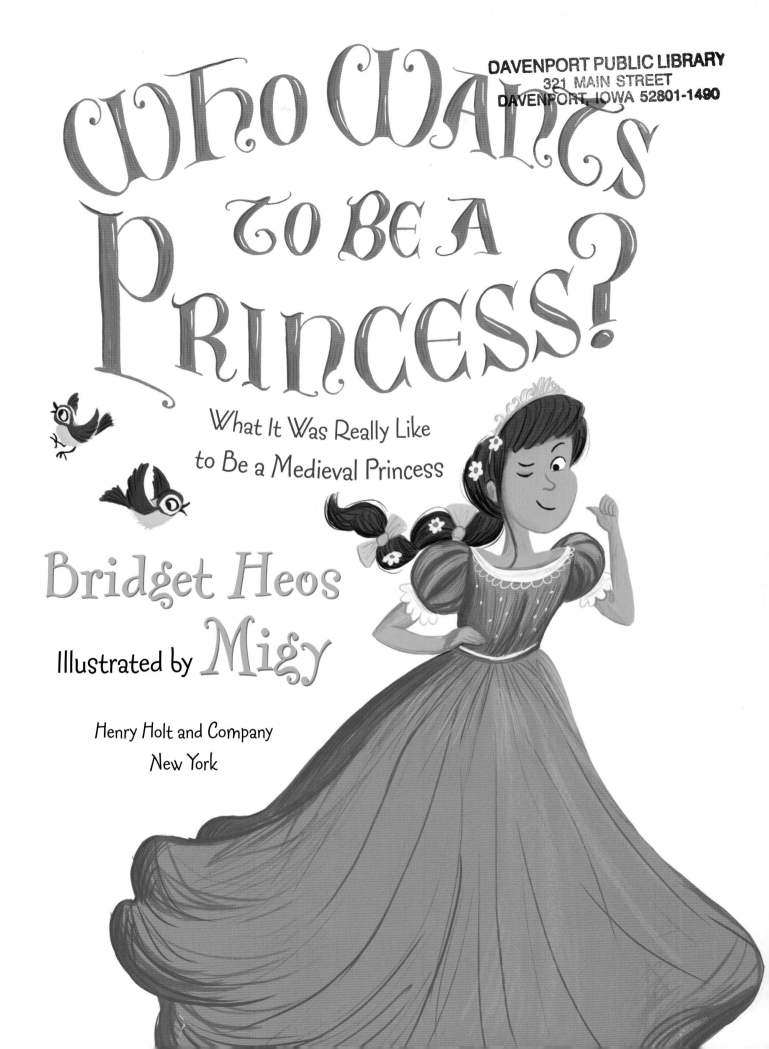

Who Wants to Be a Princess?

What It Was Really Like to Be a Medieval Princess

Bridget Heos

Illustrated by Migy

Henry Holt and Company
New York

Psst... you in your tiara and twirly dress. You look like you're dreaming of being a princess like Cinderella.

Or
Snow White.

Or
Sleeping Beauty.

But those are fairy-tale princesses. How would you like to be a **very real** princess from the Middle Ages? Like me, Beatrice. Let me tell you about my day versus a fairy-tale day.

In a fairy tale, the castle may look like this.

But my castle is plain. It's like a little village with people baking bread and brushing horses, and knights standing guard.

That smell? It's from the moat. It's full of potty water and garbage. It's perfect for keeping out unwanted visitors.

But kiss a frog that's been swimming in that water? I don't think so.

You might picture my room as pink and fluffy.

Really it's dark and made of stone. And it's not just a princess room. All the royal kids in the castle sleep here. It's like a slumber party—every day.

We don't have glass windows, only wooden shutters. In the winter, we close them tight. So we awake in darkness and dress by candlelight.

You might expect me to wear a beautiful gown.

That's only for special occasions. For ordinary days, I wear itchy wool. And no tiara. Crowns are only for really special occasions, like when my mom and dad became king and queen.

Time to start the day. In stories, girls may trot
off to Princess Charm School.

But I'm already charming. And I don't go anywhere for school.
The other royal children and I have a tutor who lives within the castle
walls. He teaches us French, *mon ami*! (That's French for "my friend.")

Now it's time to frolic in the forest. (That's princess for "play.")
I bet you think I sing—la la la la—to the forest animals and that
they sing back.

Please. This is the real world. I practice riding and archery.

Lunchtime! Finally, I get to see Mother and Father.
(They're usually busy bossing around their subjects.) You
may have seen paintings of us dining at the high table, and
we do. But our food may surprise you. It certainly does us!
We're having peacock. The cook has replaced its head
with a wild boar's head.

On the side: pies . . . filled with birds. Four and twenty blackbirds have escaped and are flying overhead. It may sound like a nursery rhyme, but the cook really makes this dish for our amusement. Huzzah!

We rarely sweep. Bones, grease, and crumbs (and now bird doo) pile up on the floor. Rats are everywhere. We'd prefer they leave, but what can we do? (Other than tidy up, I mean.)

Princess cupcakes for dessert?

If only. After lunch, we eat aged cheese. That means old cheese. It's a delicacy. (Not to mention a smell-icacy.)

By now you must be wondering: When is the fancy fairy-tale ball?
Me too!

We have dances only on holidays or when we have royal guests. On ordinary days, we do quiet things like embroider. Do you ever have quiet afternoons?

As the sun sets, we dine again. We often have visitors.

In stories, an evil queen might come to cast a dastardly spell.

But in real life, it's just traveling jugglers
and a sappy troubadour singing love songs.

One day, a prince really will sweep me away.

But he might not be charming—or handsome. I may not even know him. My parents will choose him. We'll marry when we're about twelve. I hope we like each other, even if he does look funny and act goofy.

It's dark now. At a fairy-tale park, the castle would light up the night sky. Knights would guard against dragons or evil wizards.

But we have no lights. In the darkness, people sleep everywhere.
Servants rest beside their work because they have no rooms of their
own. And the real danger is from armies who might try to overtake
our castle in the dark.

I snuggle into my bed when I'm afraid. Not a fairy-tale bed like this.

But an ordinary bed like this one.
My sister tells me a story about a
princess far, far away. I fall asleep . . .

. . . and dream of being you!

Author's Note

In this story, Princess Beatrice is a fictional medieval princess. The Middle Ages (medieval times) lasted from CE 500 to CE 1500—that's 1,000 years! A lot changed during that time. This book describes what life would have been like for a princess who lived around 1100–1300 in what is now Great Britain.

Every castle was different. But typically, a castle was a collection of buildings surrounded by castle walls. Sometimes a moat encircled the castle to discourage invading armies. As the years passed, castles became more comfortable. Still, the royalty eventually chose to live in palaces and great houses instead of drafty old castles.

Royal children like Beatrice lived at home until they were about seven. Then they might have gone to serve at another castle or, when the girls were twelve or older, to marry a prince or duke. Their parents arranged these marriages for political gain, but the princesses often had some say. Nobody wanted the prince and princess to dislike each other—though that sometimes happened!

Life as a princess was in some ways glamorous. But as you can see, there were difficulties and dangers that came with being royalty. And princesses often had to make decisions based on duty rather than on their hopes and dreams.

Bibliography

Alexandre-Bidon, Danièle, and Didier Lett. *Children in the Middle Ages.* Translated by
    Jody Gladding. Notre Dame, IN: University of Notre Dame Press, 2000.

Blackwood, Gary L. *Life in a Medieval Castle. The Way People Live.* San Diego, CA:
    Lucent Books, 2000.

Gies, Joseph, and Frances Gies. *Life in a Medieval Castle.* New York: Harper & Row, 1979.

Macaulay, David. *Castle.* Boston: Houghton Mifflin Company, 1977.

McAleavy, Tony. *Life in a Medieval Castle. English Heritage.* New York: Enchanted Lion
    Books, 2003.

Shahar, Shulamith. *Childhood in the Middle Ages.* New York: Routledge, 1990.

Turner, Ralph V. *Eleanor of Aquitaine.* New Haven, CT: Yale University Press, 2009.

For Princesses Maeve, Sami Jeanne, and Beatrice.
—B. H.

For my little princess.
—M.

Henry Holt and Company
Publishers since 1866
175 Fifth Avenue, New York, New York 10010
mackids.com

Library of Congress Cataloging-in-Publication Data
Names: Heos, Bridget, author. | Ornia-Blanco, Miguel, illustrator.
Title: Who wants to be a princess? : what it was really like to be a medieval princess / Bridget Heos ; illustrated by Migy.
Description: First edition. | New York : Henry Holt and Company, [2017] | Includes bibliographical references.
Identifiers: LCCN 2016005890 | ISBN 9780805097696 (hardcover)
Subjects: LCSH: Princesses—Europe—History—To 1500—Juvenile literature. | Middle Ages—Juvenile literature. | Europe—Kings and rulers—
History—Juvenile literature. | BISAC: JUVENILE NONFICTION / History / Medieval. | JUVENILE NONFICTION / People & Places / Europe.
Classification: LCC D107.5 .H47 2017 | DDC 305.5/22—dc23
LC record available at https://lccn.loc.gov/2016005890

Our books may be purchased in bulk for promotional, educational, or business use.
Please contact your local bookseller or the Macmillan Corporate and Premium Sales Department
at (800) 221-7945 ext. 5442 or by e-mail at MacmillanSpecialMarkets@macmillan.com.

First Edition—2017 / Designed by April Ward
The artist used a mixture of inks, paint, and digital techniques to create the illustrations for this book.
Printed in China by Toppan Leefung Printing Ltd., Dongguan City, Guangdong Province

1 3 5 7 9 10 8 6 4 2